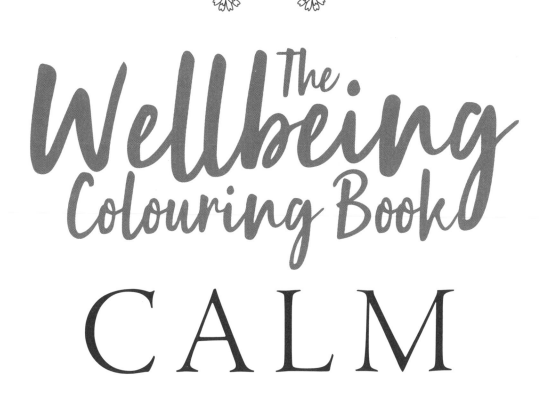

The Wellbeing Colouring Book
CALM

Michael O'Mara Books Limited

First published in Great Britain in 2022 by
Michael O'Mara Books Limited
9 Lion Yard
Tremadoc Road
London SW4 7NQ

A CIP catalogue record for this book is available from the British Library.

Papers used by Michael O'Mara Books Limited are natural, recyclable products made from wood grown in sustainable forests. The manufacturing processes conform to the environmental regulations of the country of origin.

ISBN: 978-1-78929-434-7 in paperback print format

1 2 3 4 5 6 7 8 9 10

Cover design by Ana Bjezancevic and Barbara Ward
Cover illustration by Pimlada Phuapradit
Illustrations by Angelika Scudamore, Charlotte Pepper, Felicity French, Lizzie Preston, Pimlada Phuapradit, Pope Twins

Printed and bound in China

www.mombooks.com